LEVEL 2

A learn-as-you-play tutor

PAMELA WEDGWOOD

© 1994 by Faber Music Ltd
First published in 1994 by Faber Music Ltd
3 Queen Square London WC1N 3AU
Music and Text set by Ternary Graphics
Design by Lynette Williamson
Cover Design by S&M Tucker
Cartoons © 1994 by John Levers
Printed in England by Halstan and Co Ltd
All rights reserved

ISBN 0 571 51338 7

2

QUICK REVISION

Some Reminders For Your Reference

Note and Rest Values

$\mathbf{o}$ = semibreve or whole note = 4 counts ▬

𝅗𝅥 = minim or half note = 2 counts ▬

♩ = crotchet or quarter note = 1 count 𝄽

♪ = quaver or eighth note = ½ count 𝄾

𝅘𝅥𝅯 = semiquaver or sixteenth note = ¼ count 𝄿

Simple Time Signatures

These are the simplest and most commonly used time signatures:

$\frac{4}{4}$ or (**C**) common time = 4 crotchet beats to the bar/measure

$\frac{3}{4}$ = 3 crotchet beats to the bar $\frac{2}{4}$ = 2 crotchet beats to the bar

Key Signatures

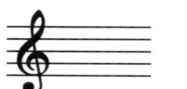 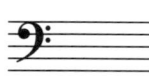        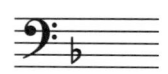

C major has no sharps or flats   G major has F sharp   F major has B flat

The Stave and Leger Lines   (notes placed above or below the stave)

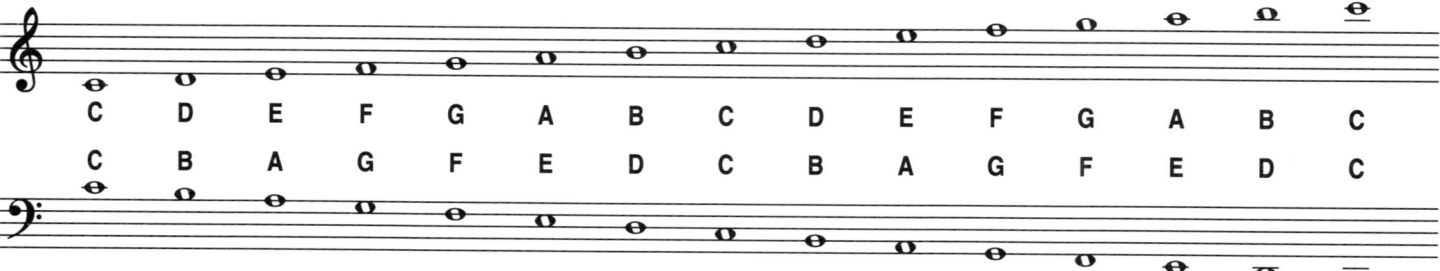

C D E F G A B C D E F G A B C
C B A G F E D C B A G F E D C

New

More Time Signatures

$\frac{4}{2}$ = 4 minim counts to the bar $\frac{4}{8}$ = 4 quaver counts to the bar

$\frac{3}{2}$ = 3 minim counts to the bar $\frac{3}{8}$ = 3 quaver counts to the bar

$\frac{2}{2}$ = 2 minim counts to the bar $\frac{2}{8}$ = 2 quaver counts to the bar

---

Compound Time Signatures – A Reminder

$\frac{6}{8}$ = 6 quaver beats to each bar

$\frac{9}{8}$ = 9 quaver beats to each bar

$\frac{12}{8}$ = 12 quaver beats to each bar

In these time signatures:

♪ = 1 beat   — rest = ♪

♩ = 2 beats   — rest = 𝄽

♩. = 3 beats   — rest = 𝄽·

𝅗𝅥. = 6 beats   — rest = ▬·

Whole bar rest ▬ in any time

Keyboard Layout

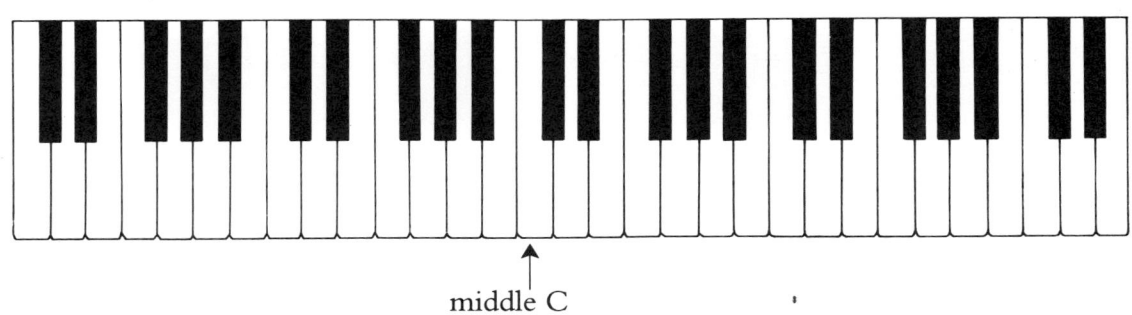

middle C

Play-it-Again Sam's EASY start to Book 2

Tied notes (add them together and hold for 4 counts)

Kum ba ya

Key – C major

African folktune

Country Gardens

Key – C major

English dance

Violin Concerto
(extract from 2nd movement)

REMINDER Using chord I, V⁷, IV

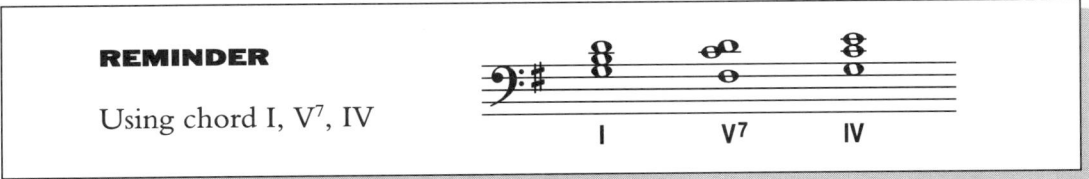

Key – G major

Beethoven

Melody's First Mini-Quiz

How many beats in this note?

What is this sign?

What type of rest is this?

What does *mf* mean?

What does ——————— mean?

Are you sitting correctly at the keyboard?

REMINDER

The first time through, play all the music under |1.

When you play the passage again leave out |1.   and play from |2.

Violin Concerto
(extract from 2nd movement)

Mendelssohn

Split Common Time

¢ = 2/2 (2 minim counts to the bar ♩)

 indicates minim count

The music should have a two-in-the-bar feel

Try the following clapping exercises:

Play-it-Again Sam's Clapping Exercises

See the Conquering Hero Comes

Adding notes in the bass clef

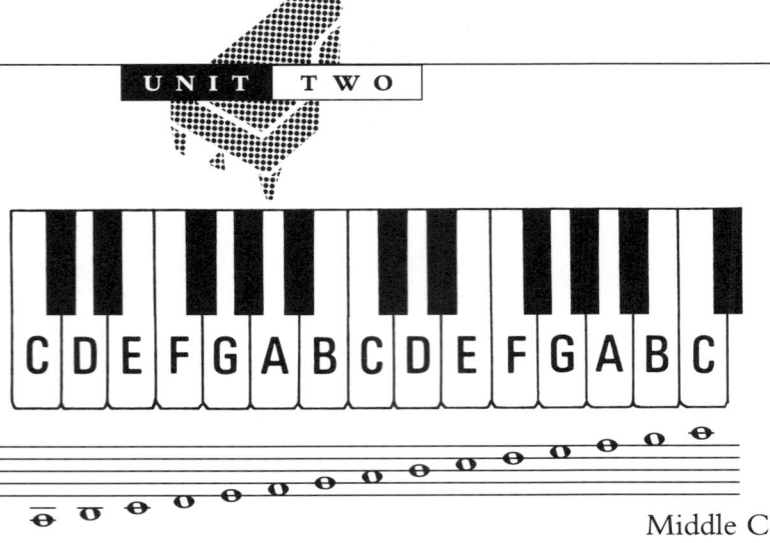

Play-it-Again Sam's 'Bassy Tunes'

The Elephant
(from 'Carnival of the Animals')

Saint Saëns

Swingin' Bass

PW

We wish you a merry Christmas

Traditional

Easy Break

Play-it-Again Sam's Sight Reading Test!

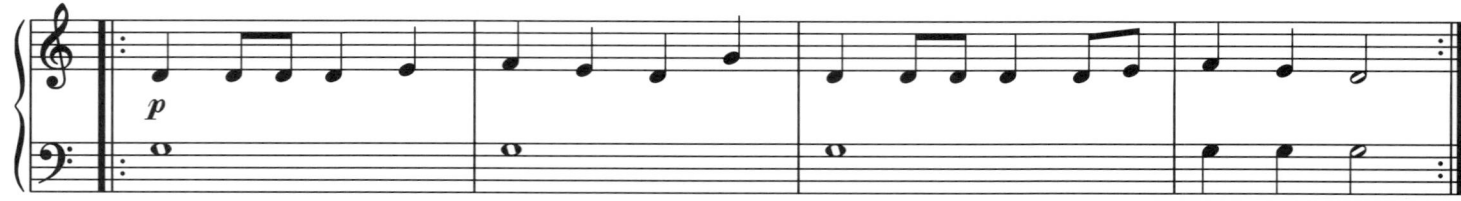

Sight Reading Test 2

Sight Reading Test 3
Don't forget F sharp!

Sight Reading Test 4
Don't forget B flat!

Hot Fingers Legato Exercise
(for 'Après la Guerre')

Après la Guerre
(French Army Song)

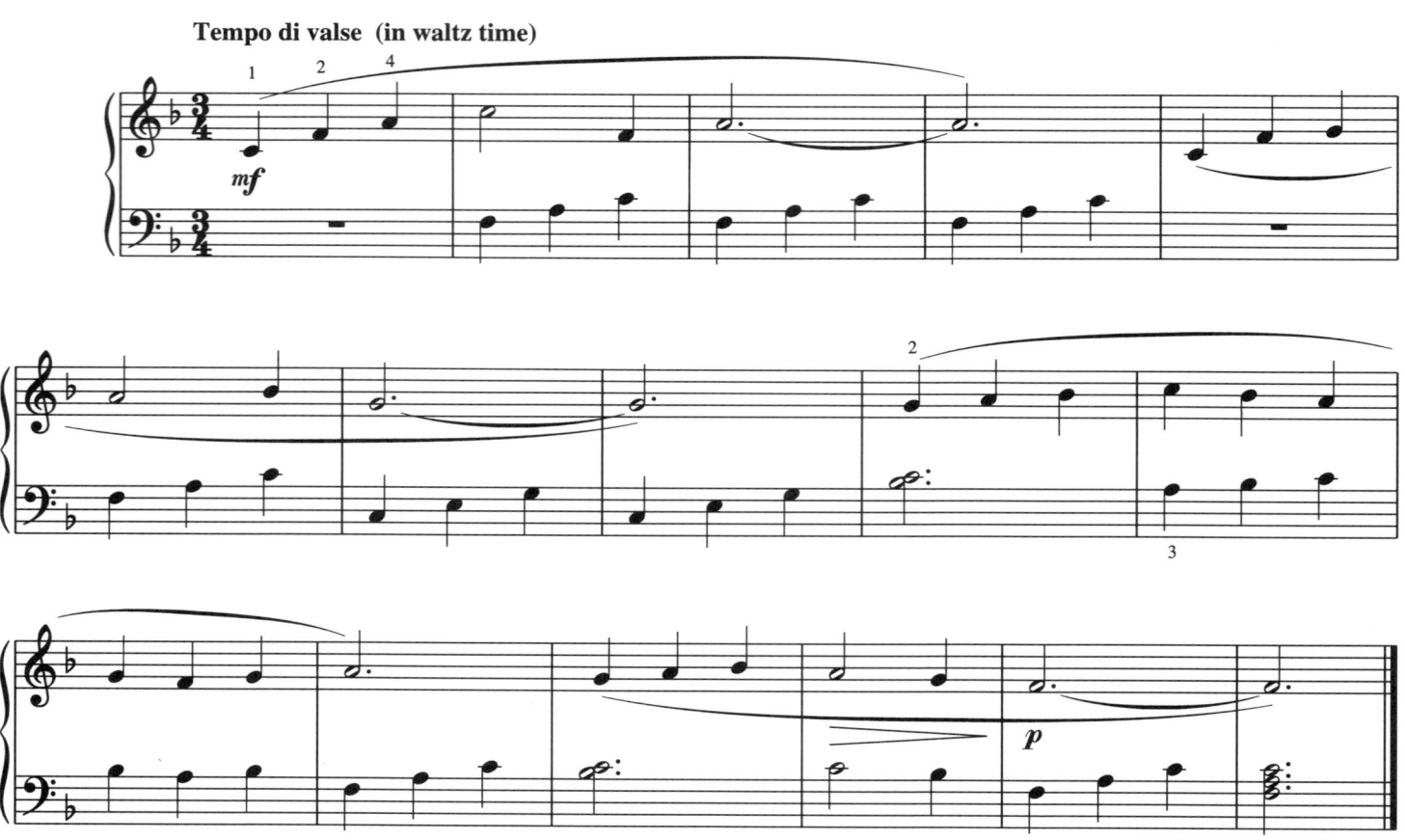

The Grasshopper and the Elephant

In march time *Bucalossi*

Melody's Stretching-Your-Musical-Knowledge Quiz

𝄵 indicates _____

What is an accidental?

𝄴 indicates _____

Name the following notes:

Finish this tune

The key of G major has _____ in its key signature

The key of F major has _____ in its key signature

Legato means _____

What does **f** indicate?

What does **p** indicate?

What does **mf** indicate?

Tempo di valse means?

Adagio means _____

Allegro means _____

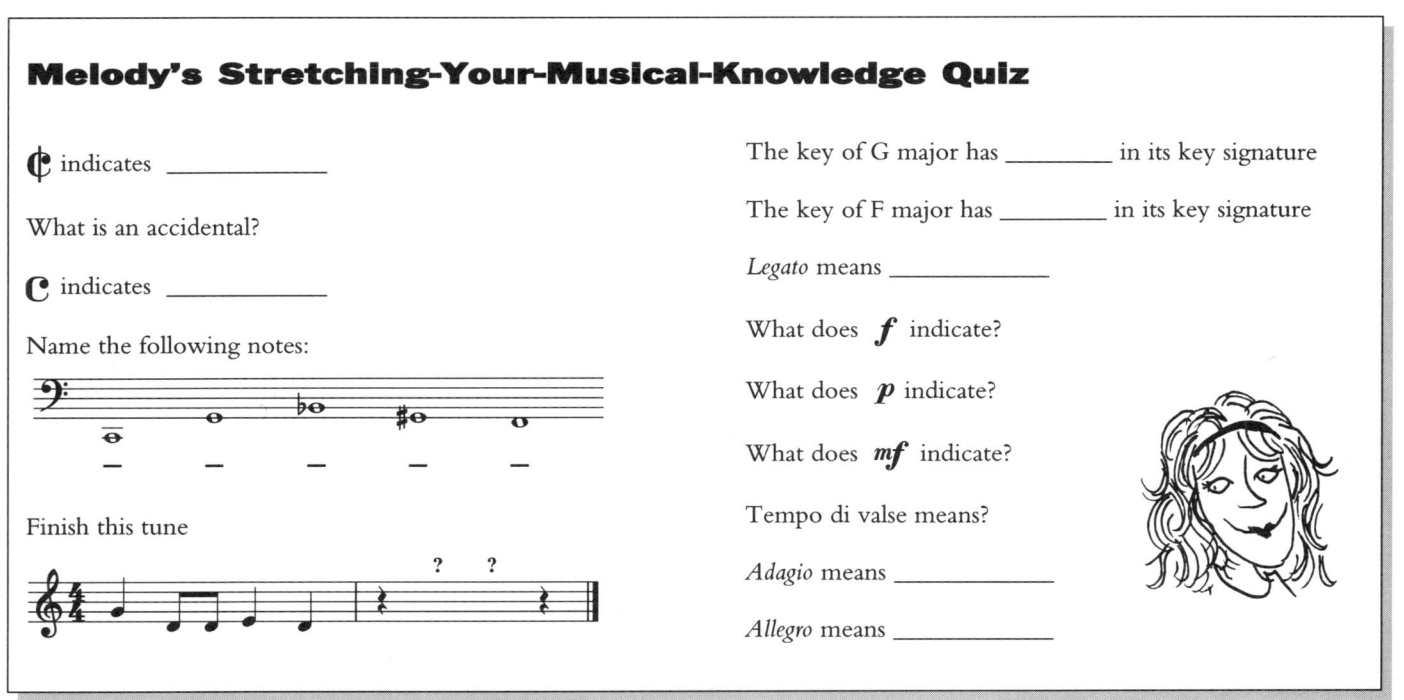

UNIT THREE

The scales of C major and A minor (play all scales up and down)

A **scale** is a succession of consecutive notes starting from any given note up or down to the next note of the same name.

Here is the scale of C major

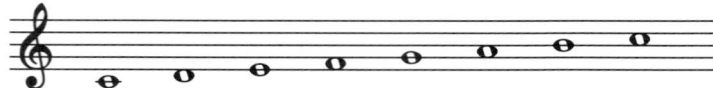

Tones and **semitones** are used to establish the correct pattern.

Some notes are a **semitone** (half a step) apart

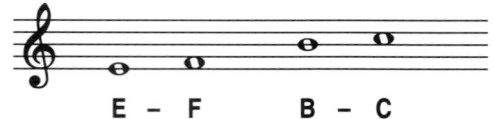

Some notes are a **whole tone** (a whole step) apart

The pattern of every major scale is:

C major scale

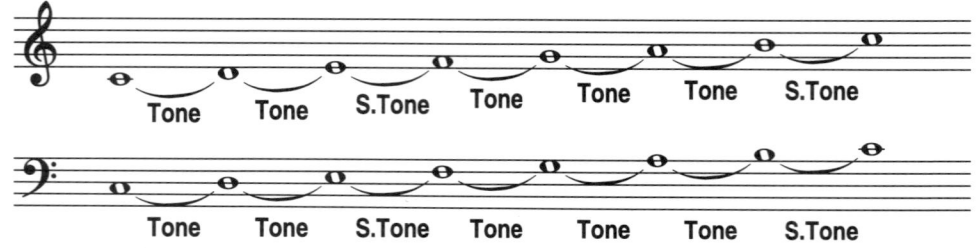

Work at each hand separately – then play together

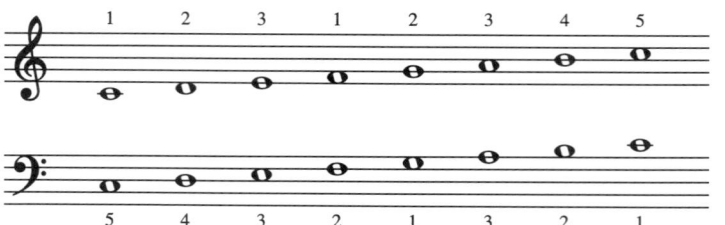

C major scale over 2 octaves

RH

LH

A Scaley Passage

Scaling Down to Size

Every major key has a **Relative Minor**

You can find the relative minor by counting down three half-steps (**semitones**) from the key-note of the major scale.

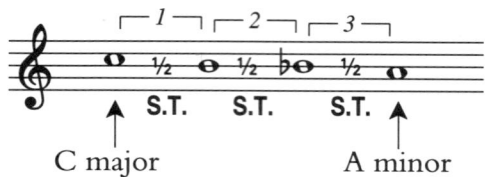

Another way - the Relative Minor uses the 6th note of the major scale for its starting note:

C major

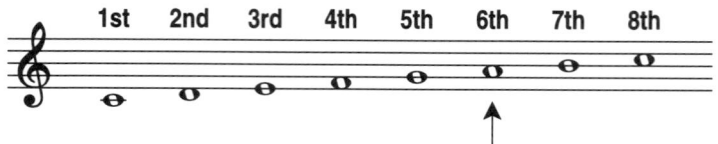

The key signatures of C major and A minor are the same

The pattern of tones and semitones for the **Harmonic Minor** scale are:

A harmonic minor

G sharp is an accidental in the key of A minor.
It is **not** in the key signature

It is necessary to **raise** the 7th note to **G sharp** in order to make a semitone interval

A harmonic minor scale (play all scales up *and* down)

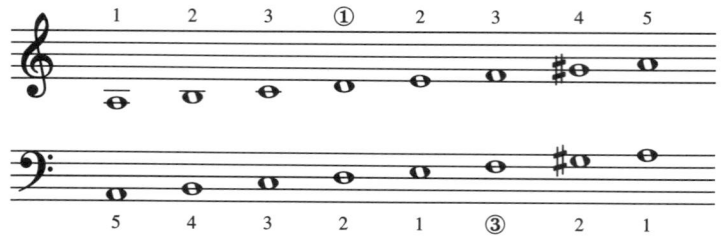

Work at each hand separately - then together

A harmonic minor scale (over 2 octaves)

Play-it-Again Sam's Study in A minor

A changing gear exercise!

Why do we have minor keys?

The minor key produces a much duller sound – a bit SAD!
The major key produces a much brighter sound – CHEERFUL!

Key – A minor

Melody's 'All is Lost' Song

UNIT FOUR

Hot Fingers Chord Warm-ups in A minor

I   IV   I   V7   I

Play-it-Again-Sam's Piano Concerto
(borrowed from E. Grieg)

REMINDER — accent the note

More Compound Time

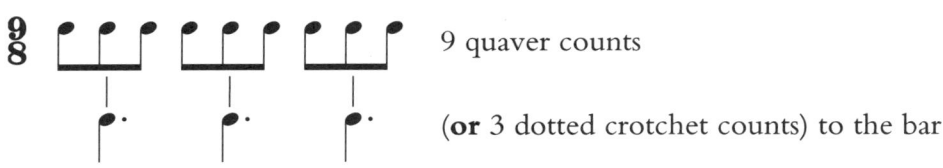

9 quaver counts

(**or** 3 dotted crotchet counts) to the bar

Play-it-Again Sam's Clap and Count Exercise

Play-it-Again Sam's Workout

Play slowly

Jesu, joy of Man's Desiring

J.S.Bach
arr. PW

Moderato

A Winter's Tale

With a good lilt

PW

D.S. al CODA   Go back to the sign 𝄋 (Dal Segno) until you reach ⊕, then go to CODA.
CODA   The bit on the end.

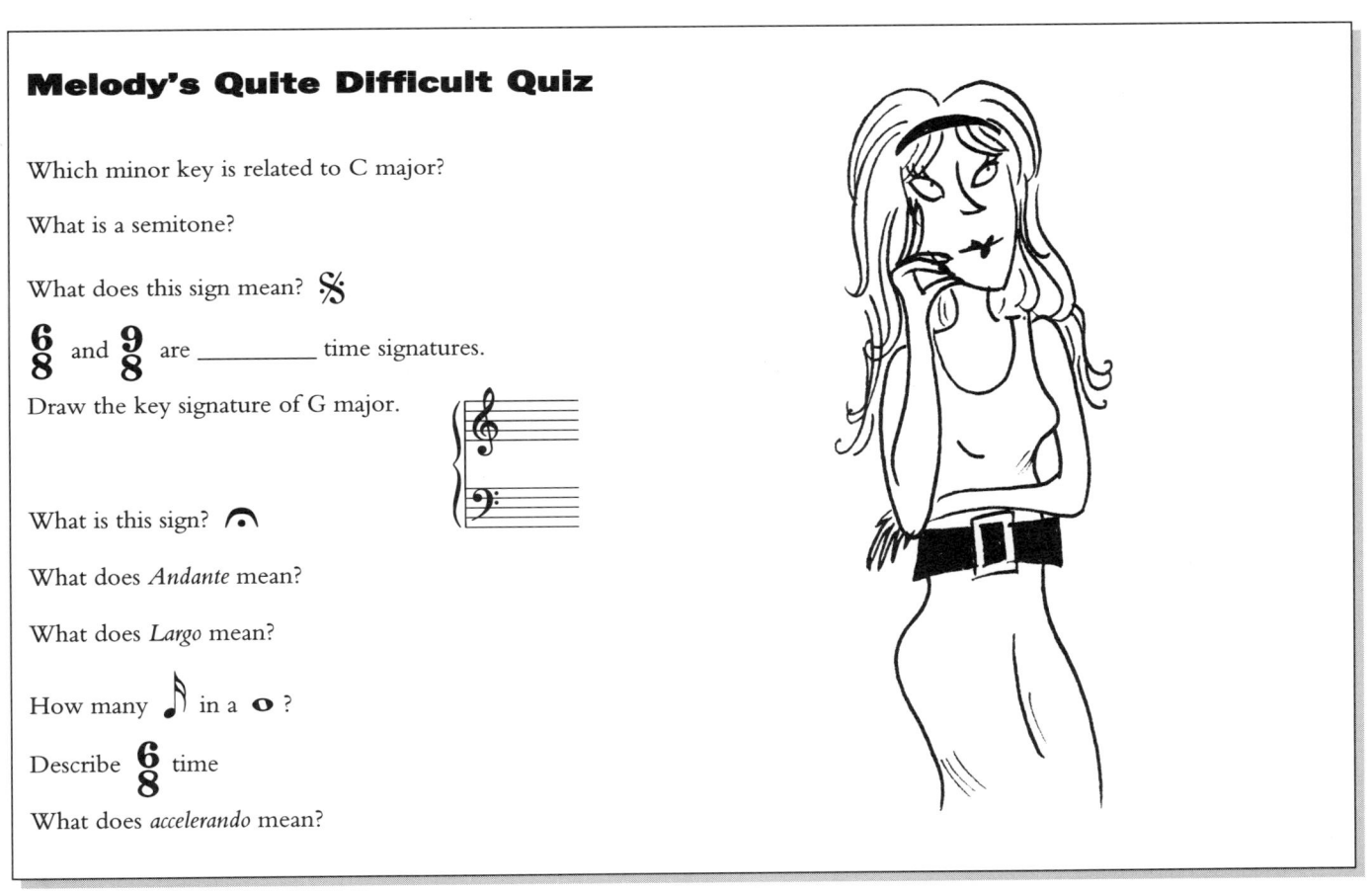

The scale of G major

(play all scales up *and* down)

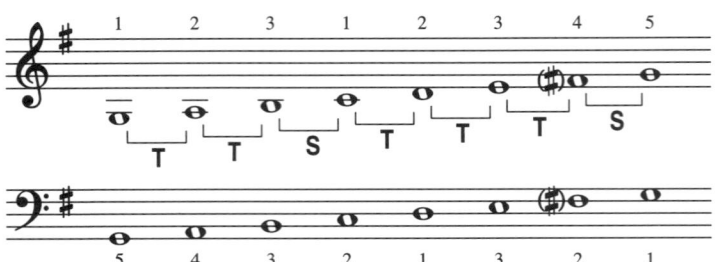

Work at each hand separately, then together

G major scale over 2 octaves

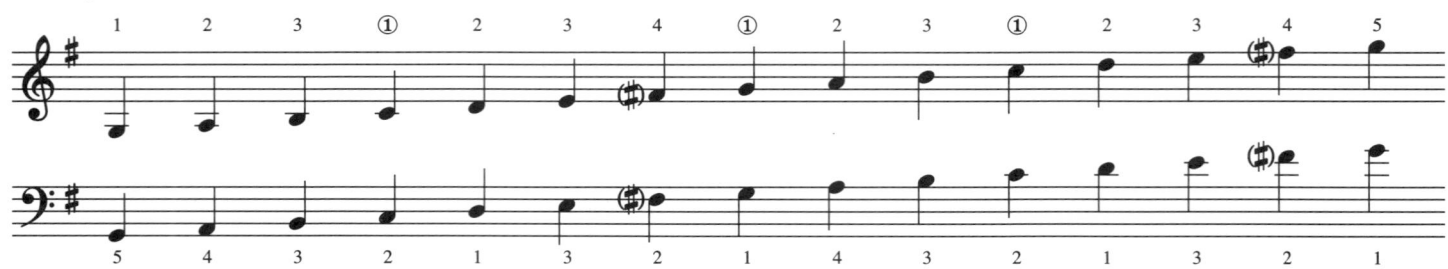

REMINDERS

The key signature in the key of G major

Accent the note

Hot Left-Hand Fingers Study in G major

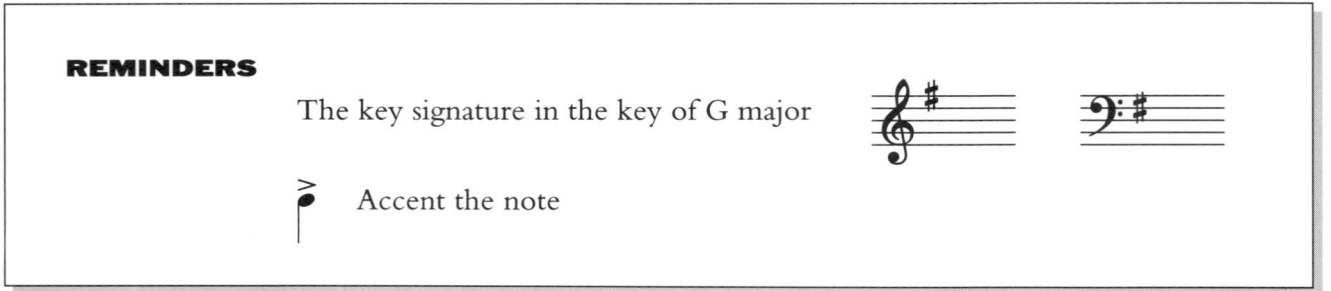

A Quiet Moment

PW

Sunday Morning

PW

O Sole Mio

Moderato

Rinaldo Di Capua, arr. PW

Melody's Fun Page

A Try-not-to-panic Sight Reading Test!

Try to complete these well-known tunes:

Westminster Chimes

Old MacDonald

Auld Lang Syne

Now compose your **own** melody in the following keys/times
Don't forget to add the correct key signature!

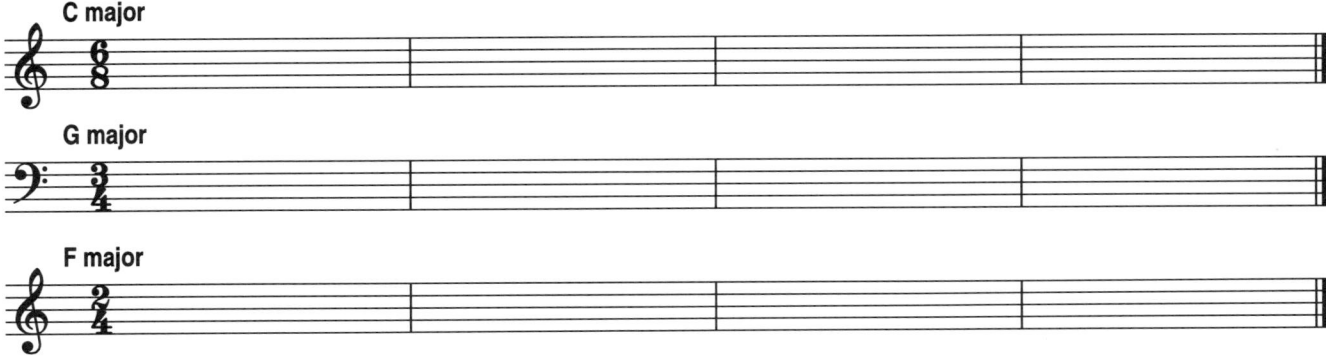

C major

G major

F major

Bridge Street Boogie

Bass: A C E G
G B D F A

UNIT SIX

The relative minor of G major is E MINOR

E Harmonic Minor Scale (play all scales up *and* down)

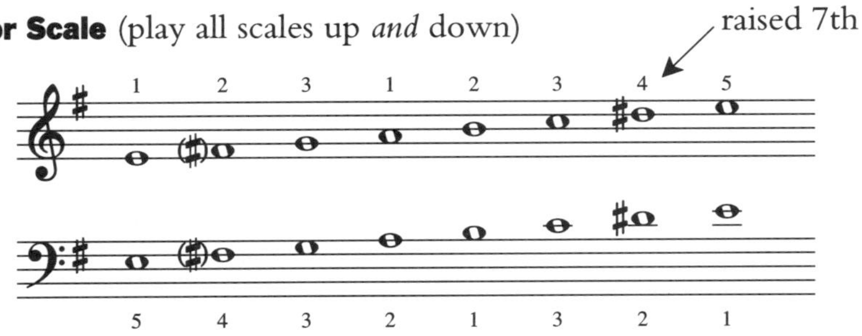

Play first with hands separately, then together

E Harmonic Minor over 2 octaves

Hot Finger Study in E minor

Play-it-Again Sam's Left-Hand Workout
(for 'A Minor Situation')

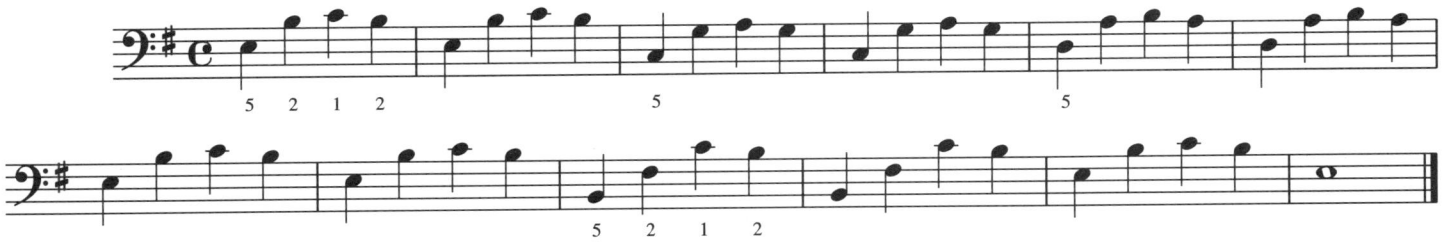

Playing chords in different positions

So far you have learnt to play chords in ROOT POSITION

Here is **Chord I** in the key of **E minor**

   Root Position

Chord I in **1st inversion** (with the 3rd note of the scale at the bottom)

Chord I in **2nd inversion** (with the 5th note of the scale at the bottom)

Now write and try to play the following **1st inversion chords** in the following keys:

Key of C major   Key of G major   Key of F major   Key of A minor

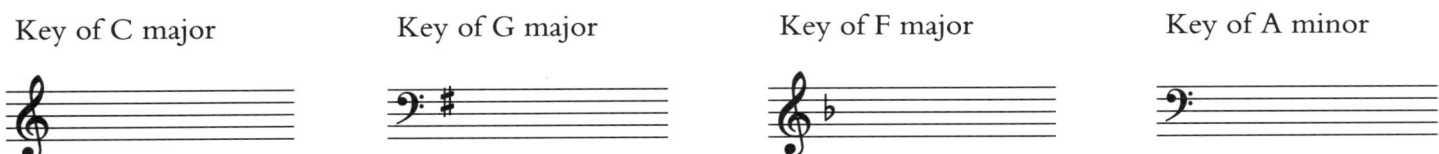

Now try to play 2nd inversion chords in the above keys.

Hot Fingers Broken-Chord Warm-Ups

Play separate hands only – follow all fingerings!

Play **Legato**

Key of C major

Key of G major

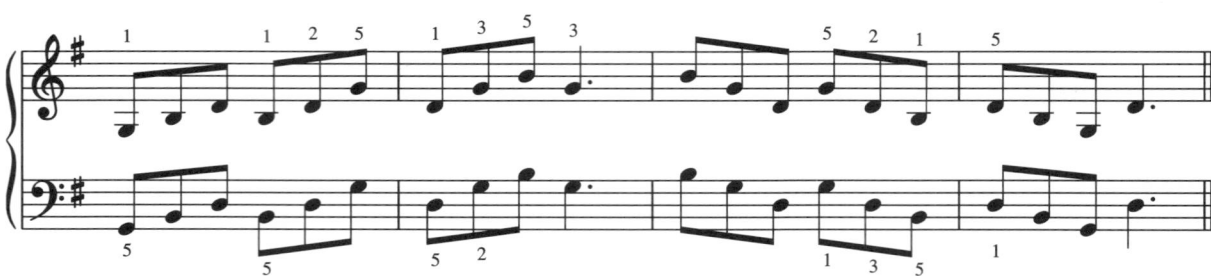

Key of F major

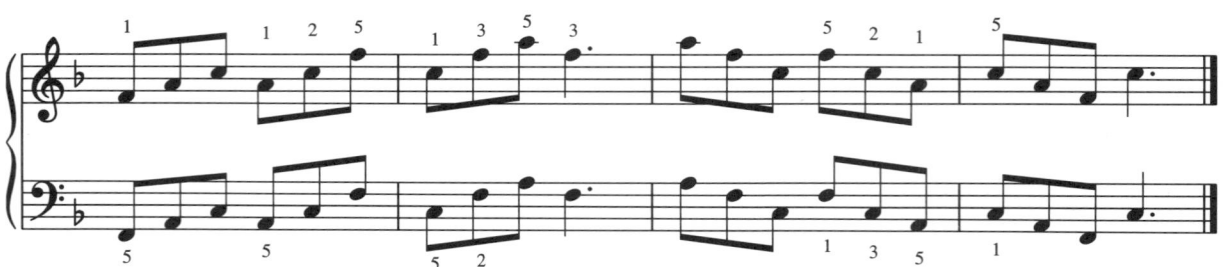

Key of A minor

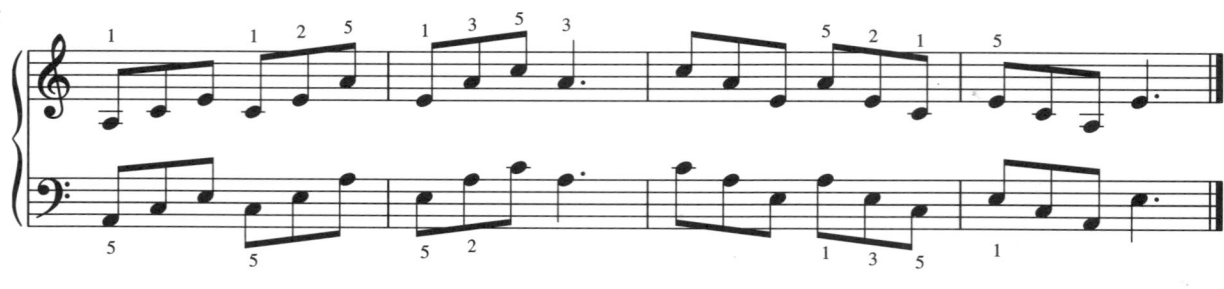

Key of E minor

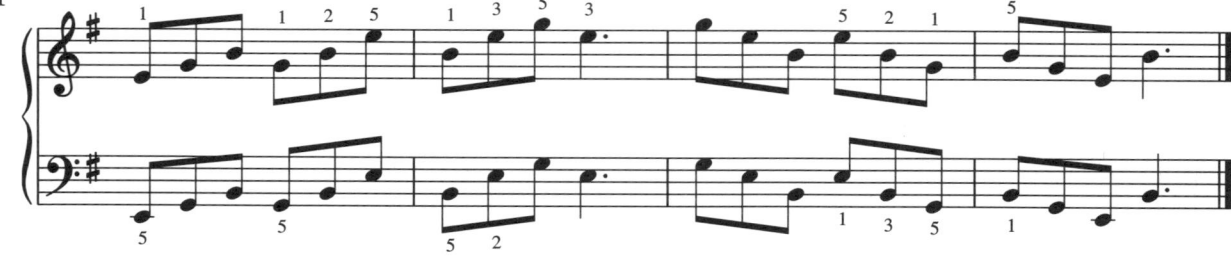

Play-it-Again Sam's Chord Reference Chart

Chords in root position, 1st and 2nd inversions

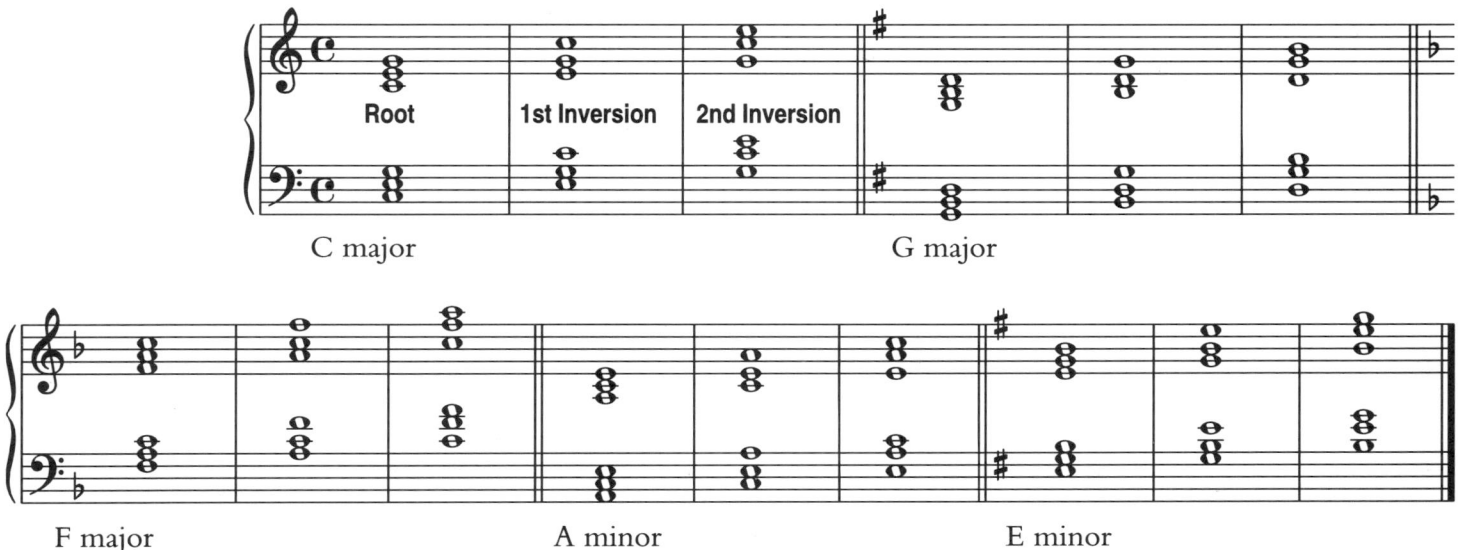

Broken Chord Blues

34

UNIT SEVEN

Adding 4/2 and 3/2 time signatures

When you see **2** as the lower figure you are counting in **minims** (half notes)

4/2 ♩♩♩♩ = 4 minim (half note) counts to the bar   3/2 ♩♩♩ = 3 minim (half note) counts to the bar

REMINDER   2/2 or ¢ split common time = 2 minim (half note) counts to the bar

Play-it-Again Sam's Finger Puzzles   Play legato – no gaps!

Hornpipe from 'The Water Music'

Handel

Theme from 'Abdelazar'

Purcell

'Spring' from 'The Four Seasons'

Vivaldi

Il est né, le divin enfant

Old French carol

Melody's Quick Time Quiz

C indicates?

4/2 time means?

6/8 time means?

9/8 time means?

3/2 time means?

2/4 time means?

2/2 time means?

¢ indicates?

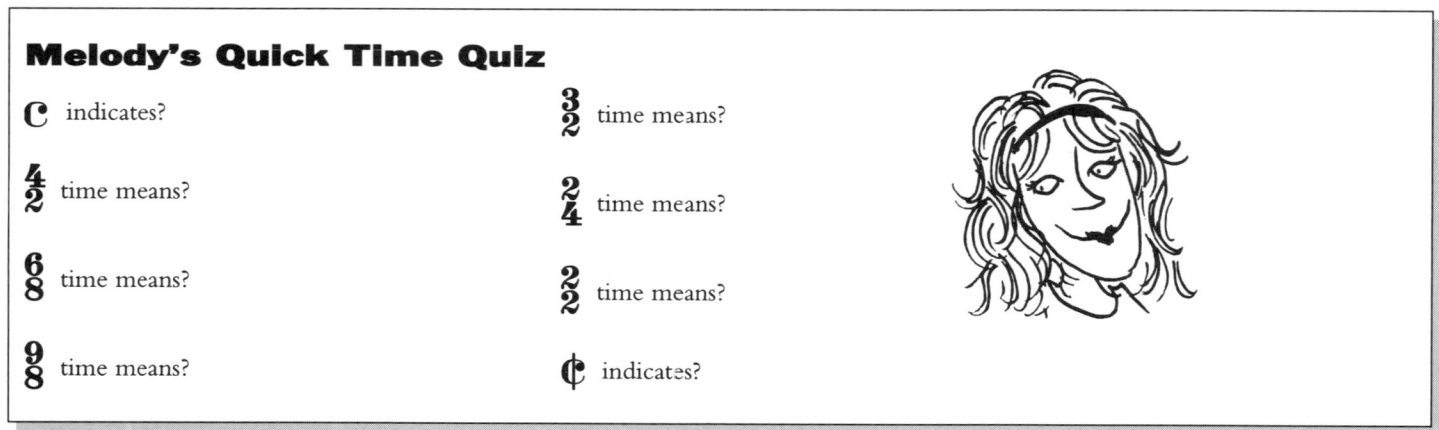

Christmas Cracker No. 1

While Shepherds Watched Their Flocks

Sarabande

Quite slow

Handel

Melody's Note-Finding Test

Find these notes on the keyboard **quickly**.

If you have scored 30 or more, WELL DONE!   Score =

UNIT EIGHT

F major scale

(play all scales up *and* down)

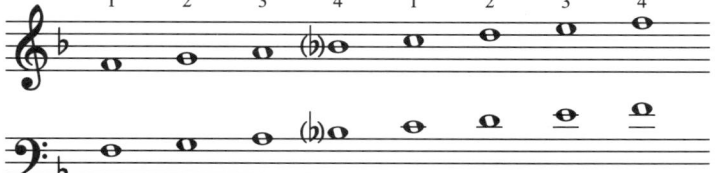

Work at each hand separately, then together

F major scale over 2 octaves

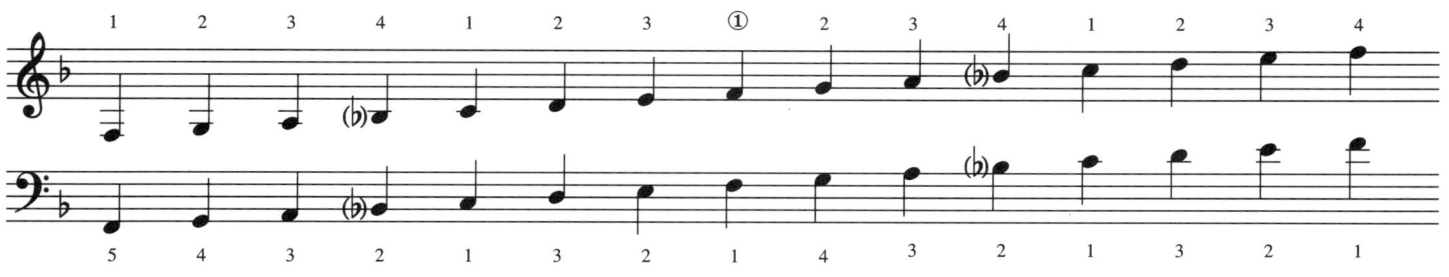

REMINDER The key-signature of F major is

Hot Fingers Strikes Again

PW

Melody's 'Guess the Tune' Time

Can you complete these well-known tunes?

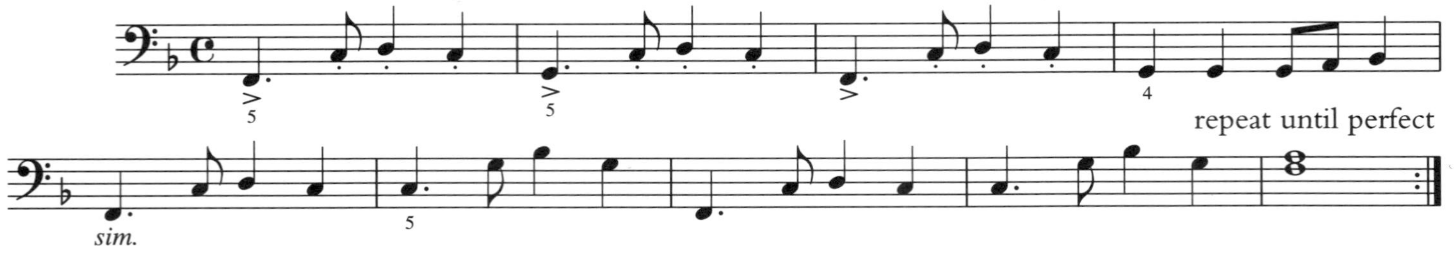

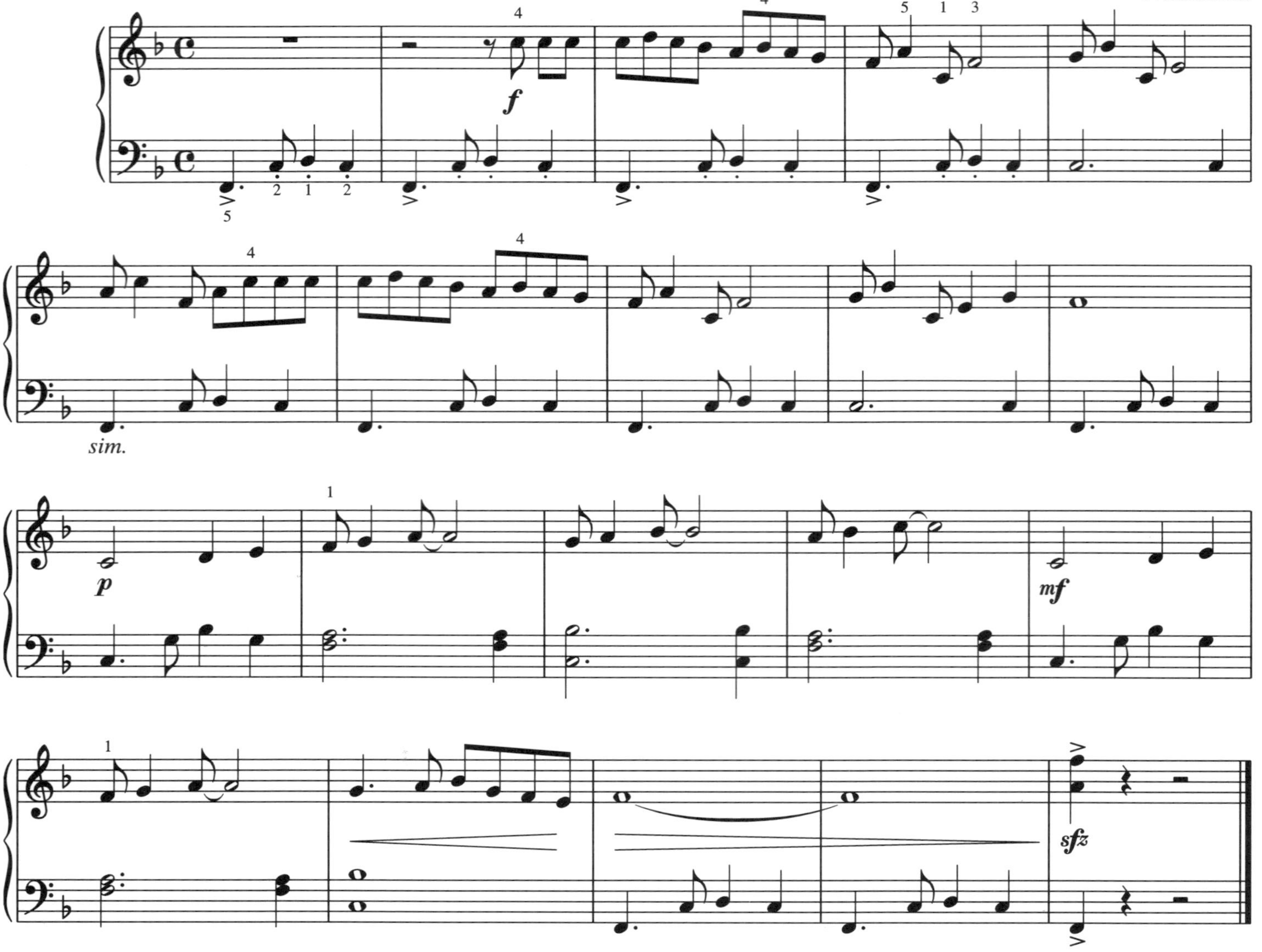

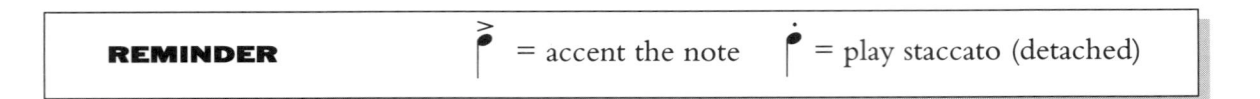

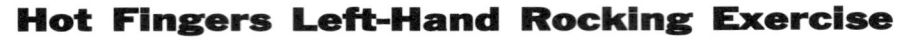

Londonderry Air (Danny Boy)

Irish Traditional, arr. PW

'Autumn' from 'The Four Seasons'

Allegro

Vivaldi, arr. PW

Haymaking

Moderato

18th-century anon, arr. PW

Melody's Boosting-Your-Confidence Tips

Can you play the major scales of C, G and F?

Can you remember which accidental belongs to the key of G major?

Can you play your BROKEN CHORD patterns without any mistakes?

Can you play any of your favourite pieces from MEMORY?

If you find any of these difficult, DON'T WORRY, keep thinking ONWARDS!

Just think how little you were able to do six months ago!

Do you seize up when playing to an audience? Most people do, so DON'T WORRY

Making regular cassette recordings of yourself will make you realize how much you have progressed, and will give you more confidence in performance. YOU ARE DOING WELL!

UNIT NINE

The Relative Minor of F major is D MINOR

D Harmonic Minor Scale (play all scales up *and* down)

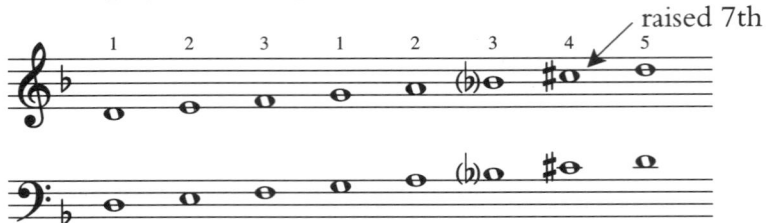

Practise hands separately, then together

D Harmonic Minor over 2 octaves

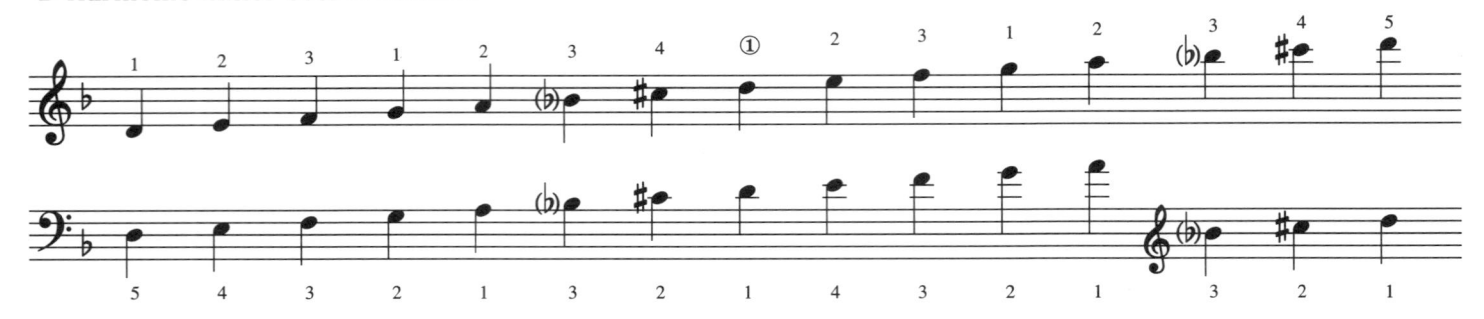

Hot Fingers in D minor

Melody's Mini Quiz

What does cantabile mean?

What is this rest ▬ worth in 3/2?

What is the relative major of D minor?

Which note is the raised 7th in D minor?

Andante Semplice

Cantabile

A. Corelli

In the Hall of the Mountain King
(from Peer Gynt)

Moderato

Grieg

Root, 1st and 2nd inversion chords in D minor

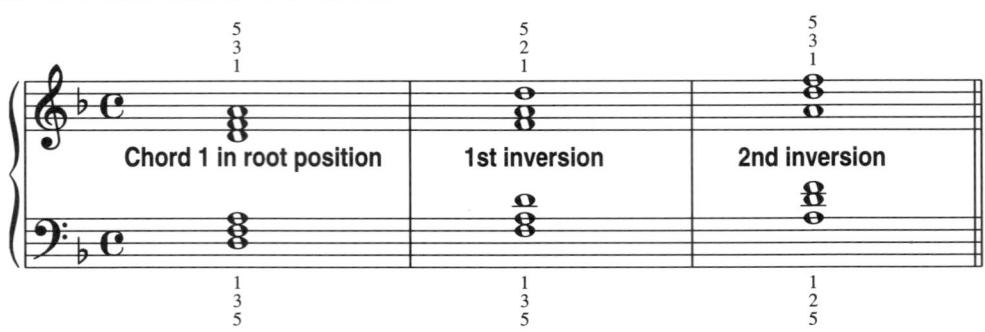

Broken Chords in D Minor

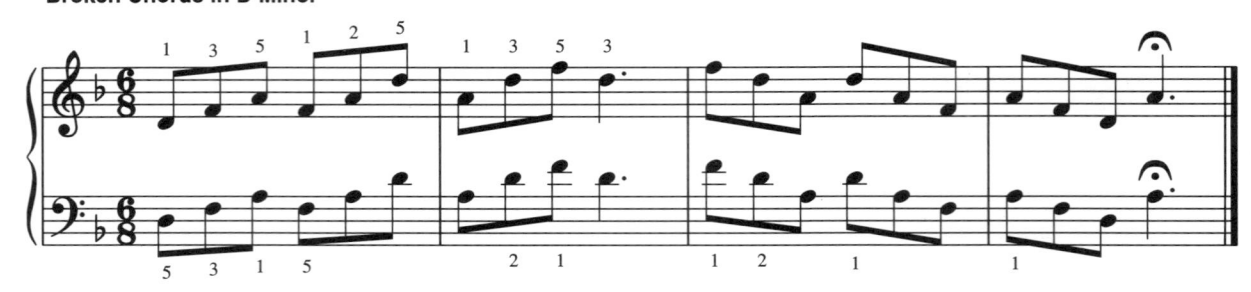

The Chase - Hot Fingers Concert Study

⊕ CODA

Melody's Reasonably Quick Quiz

The relative minor of F major is?

How many ♪'s in a ♩. ?

E minor is the relative of which major key?

What does 6/8 time mean?

mp means?

Caprice No.24

Bright

Paganini

Melody's Fun Sight-Reading Page

Play each tune **very slowly**, and try to get it right!

Christmas Cracker No. 2

Good King Wenceslas

arr. PW

Greensleeves

English traditional, arr. PW

UNIT TEN

TRIPLET REMINDER

A group of 3 notes played in the time of 2 of the same kind is called a TRIPLET

Play-it-Again Sam's Clapping Rhythm

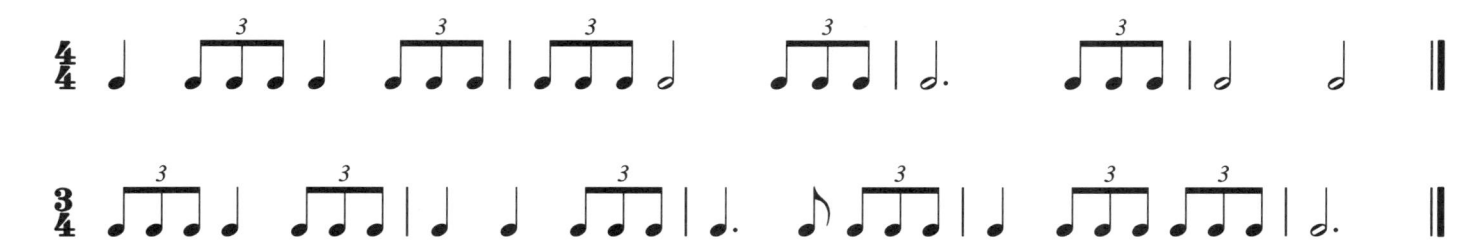

Triumphal March from 'Aïda'

Tempo di marcia

Verdi

Hot on the Line

PW

The Lark in the Clear Air

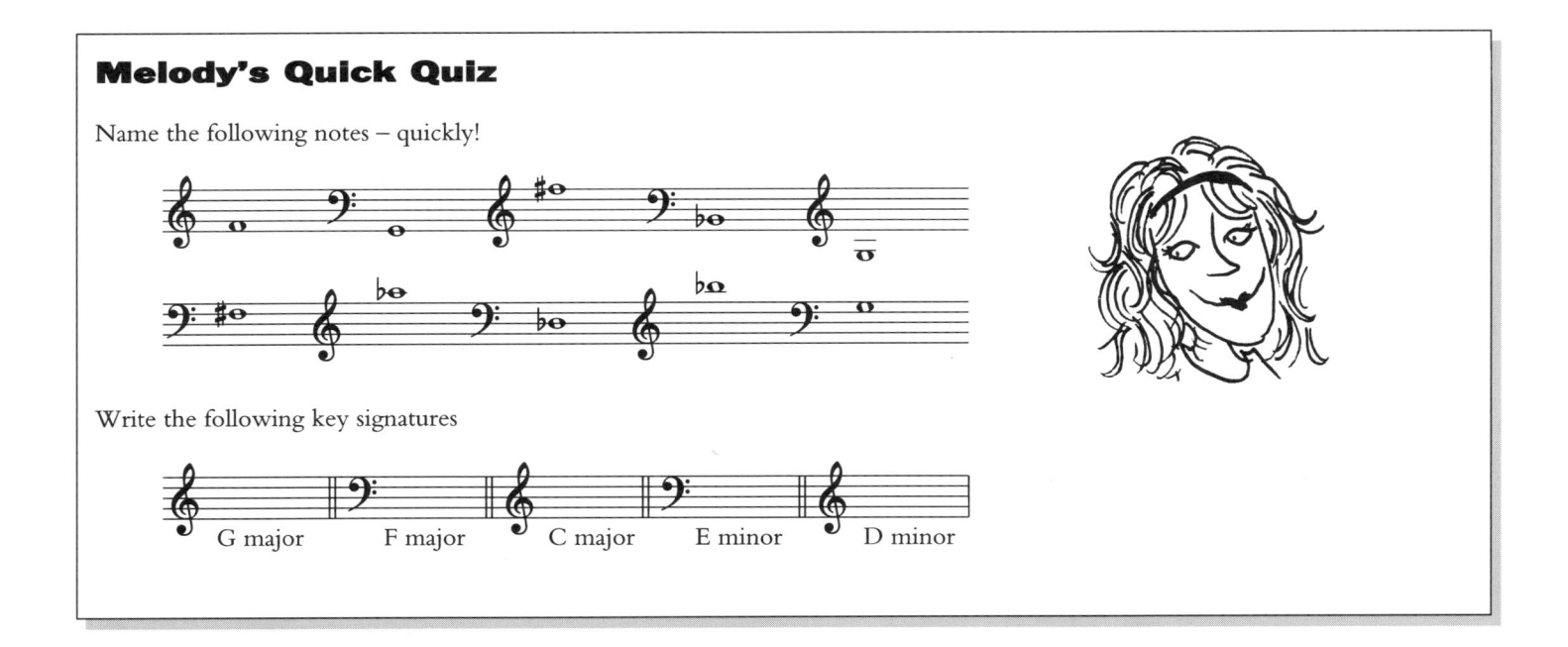

Andante

anon.

Melody's Quick Quiz

Name the following notes – quickly!

Write the following key signatures

G major   F major   C major   E minor   D minor

UNIT ELEVEN

Fascinatin' Rhythms
Play-it-Again Sam's Syncopated Clapping Exercises

Ragtime Calk Walk

Now Try these

The Entertainer

Our Little House

Play-it-Again Sam's Rhythm Exercise

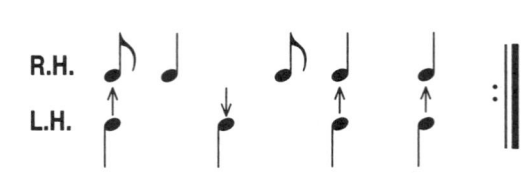

Ragtime Cake Walk: Alabama Dream

Moderato

G. Barnard

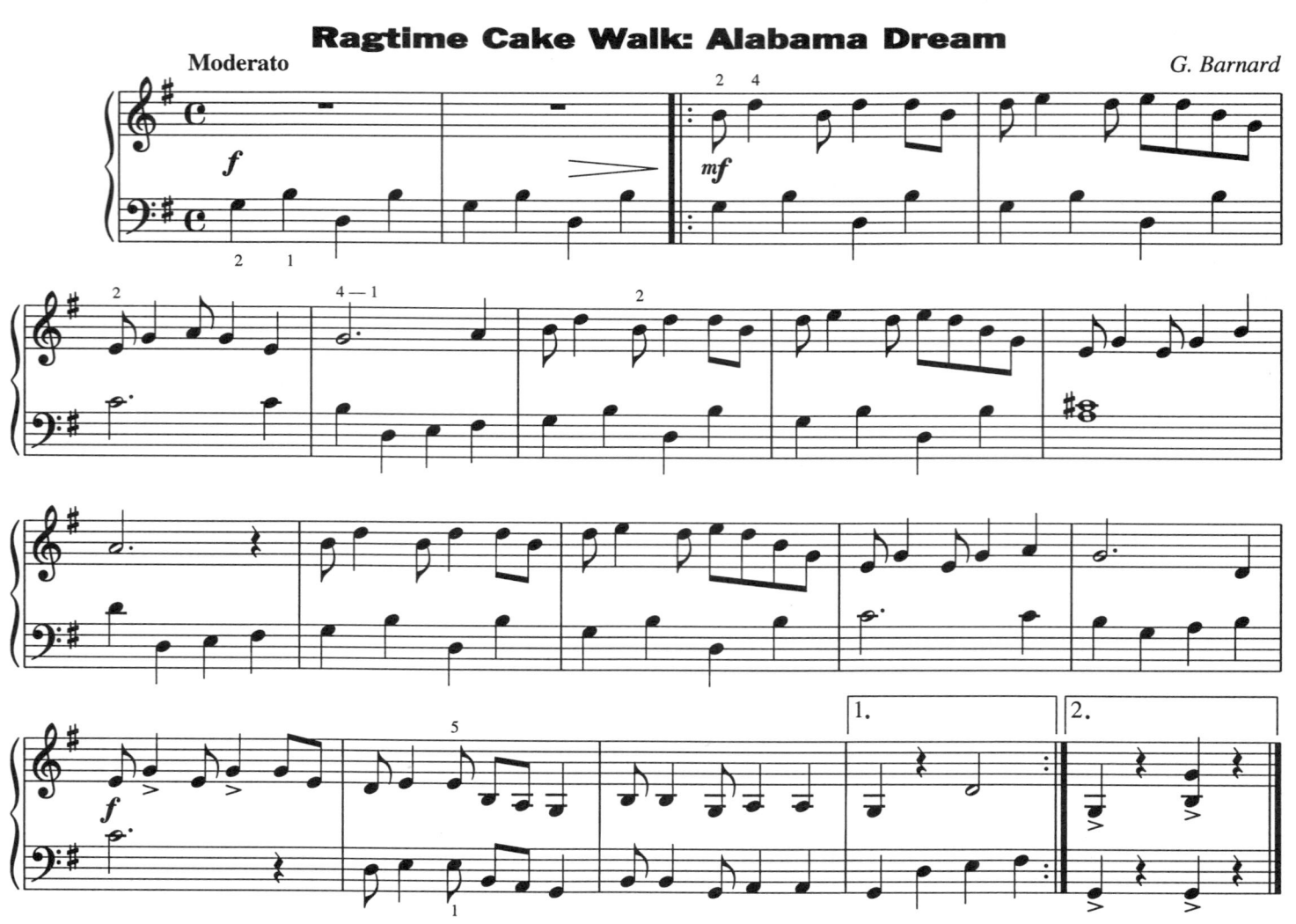

The Entertainer

When you see this sign, play 1 octave (8 notes) higher than written

Moderate speed

Scott Joplin, arr. PW

Scott Joplin (1868 – 1917) was an American composer best-known for his popular piano rags

Our Little House

UNIT TWELVE

D MAJOR has two sharps in its key signature –
F sharp and **C sharp**

D major scale (play all scales up *and* down)

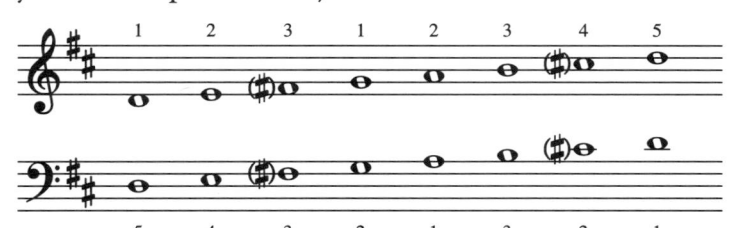

Work at each hand separately, then together

D major scale over 2 octaves

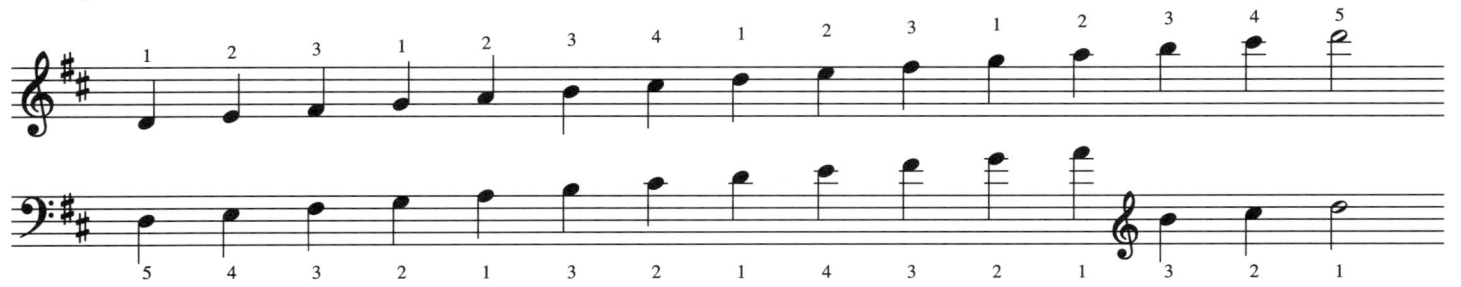

Melody's gentle start in D major

Plaisir d'amour

Padre Martini

Gently
mp
p
pp

Root, 1st and 2nd inversion chords in D major

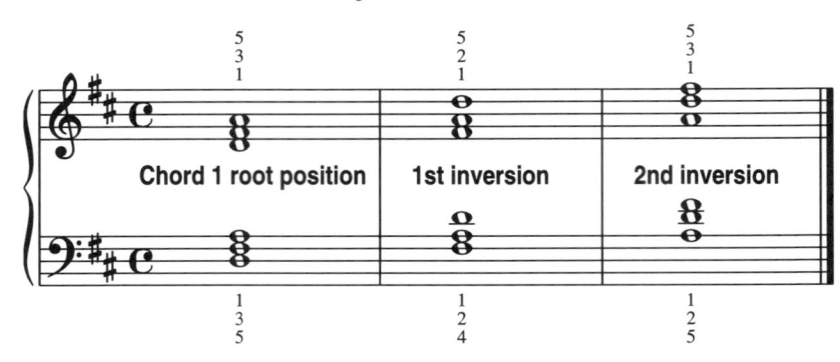

This type of broken chord is called an **arpeggio**. It uses notes 1, 3 and 5 of the scale.

D.C. Go back to the beginning. End at **FINE**.

Hot Fingers Workout in D major

At a steady tempo

Policeman's Song
(from 'The Pirates of Penzance')

Allegro non troppo — fast but not too fast!

Sullivan

Melody's Jogging-Your-Memory Quiz

What does **C** at the beginning of the stave mean?
Which minor key has 1 sharp in it?
4/2 means?
Name the notes of chord I in D major.

What does *8va* above the stave indicate?
Who was Scott Joplin?
Who wrote *Aïda*?
What does **9/8** time mean?

The Pedals

Most PIANOS have 2 or 3 pedals. Electric keyboards and pianos may also have pedal attachments.

SOFT PEDAL

SOSTENUTO PEDAL (usually only on grand pianos. Not for beginners!)

SUSTAINING PEDAL

The right (**sustaining**) pedal is sometimes improperly called the 'loud pedal'. When the pedal is used, the dampers are lifted off the strings, leaving them to resonate freely

When you see this sign ℘ed. use the sustaining pedal

When you see this sign ✱ release the sustaining pedal

The left pedal (**una corda** = 1 string) makes the sound more muted.
On an upright piano, using this pedal moves the hammers nearer to the strings, so that they strike less powerfully.
On a grand piano, using this pedal moves the whole keyboard sideways, leaving one string of each set unstruck

---

Tips Most beginners overdo the sustaining pedal.

Use your ears. Wait until you can hear the next chord – THEN USE THE PEDAL

It takes LOTS of hard work and listening!

Try these simple pedalling exercises:

Hot Foot No.1

℘ed. pedal down on the 2nd beat of each bar

✱ pedal up

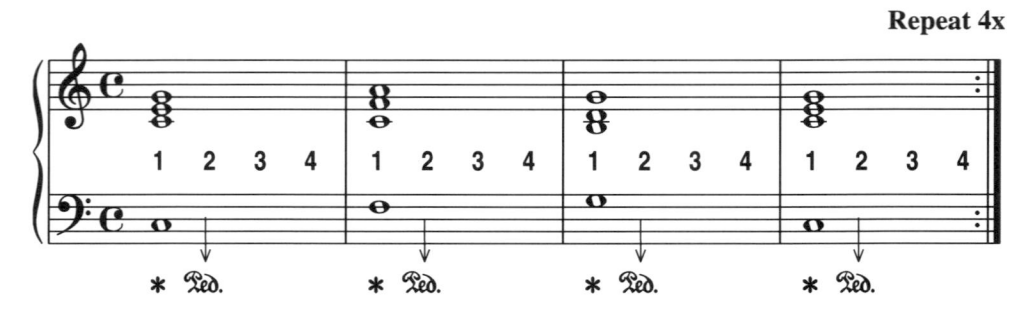

Repeat 4x

Hot Foot Pedalling Study

PLAY-IT-AGAIN SAM'S ITALIAN TERM REMINDER

ff = *fortissimo* = very loud

f = *forte* = loud

mf = *mezzo forte* = moderately loud

pp = *pianissimo* = very soft

p = *piano* = soft

mp = *mezzo piano* = moderately soft

cresc. (*crescendo*) ⎯⎯⎯ getting louder

dim. (*diminuendo*) ⎯⎯⎯ getting softer

rall. (*rallentando*) getting gradually slower

rit. (*ritenuto*) holding back the speed

poco = a little

moto = motion, movement

Largo = slow, stately

Adagio = slow

Andante = at a walking speed

Allegro = quick, cheerful

Allegretto = fairly quick, but not so quick as *Allegro*

Moderato = at a moderate speed

D.S. (*Dal Segno* 𝄋) al *FINE* = from the sign 𝄋 to *FINE* (end)

D.C. (*Da Capo*) al *FINE* = back to the beginning and go on to *FINE*

UNIT THIRTEEN

Hot Fingers Workout (for 'Für Elise')

Hot Fingers Slurred Couplet Study
(Workout for 'Dance of the Hours')

Accent the first of each pair of notes. Lift the second off lightly with an upward movement of the wrist.

THINK DOWN – UP FOR EACH GROUP

Hot Fingers Concert Repertoire
Für Elise

Beethoven, arr. PW

Dance of the Hours
(from 'La Gioconda')

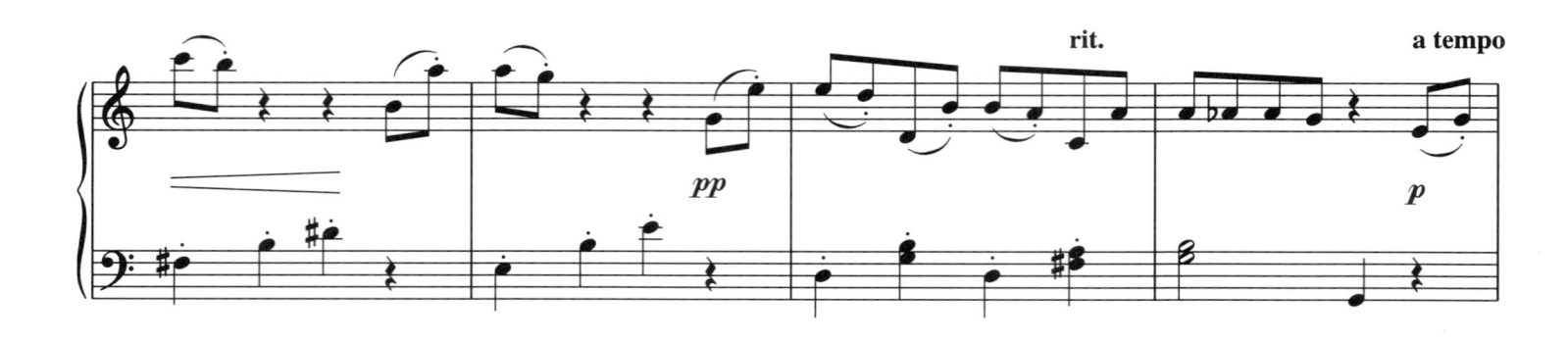

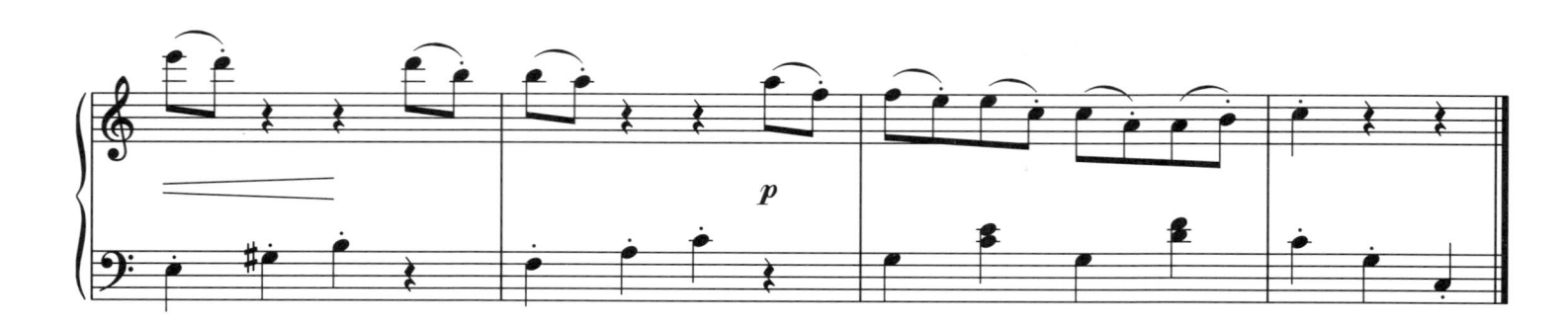

Ponchielli, arr. PW

Con grazia

Reflections

It's never too late to Charleston